More than a Schnitzel

Comfort food from a German kitchen

Christopher & Catherine Knuth

More than a Schnitzel

Comfort food from a German kitchen

NEW HOLLAND

Christopher & Catherine Knuth

*To all who love and appreciate
good German food—enjoy.*

MCVC

CONTENTS

Introduction

My parents returned to Germany after a twelve-year absence, when I was three. We settled in Blankenese, a picturesque and somewhat genteel town on the outskirts of Hamburg, on the Elbe river. It has a long history as a fishing village and it was there that I spent my childhood and early adulthood. Growing up, there was always plenty to do: from fishing and sailing on the Elbe River, to hiking and bike riding with friends in the nearby forest, where we would often try to feed the wild pigs!

Blankenese's and Hamburg's culinary specialties are various types of fish, crab, herring and eel, usually seasoned with numerous spices, in particular paprika, cayenne, cumin and bay leaves. However, game, such as deer and wild pig, are also popular as well as schnitzel—one of Germany's most famous food exports. Growing up near the sea within a close-knit farming community, my interest in produce and cooking was a natural progression. But first and foremost, I was inspired by my mother, who always took the time to cook hearty, seasonal meals for my brother and I. Sundays were a day of baking at our house in Blankenese. My mother would cook my favourite cakes like *Rotweinkuchen* (Red Wine Cake) and *Schokoladenkuchen* (Chocolate Cake). We often had so much food left over we'd invite the neighbours in and it would always become quite the party. It was also during our baking Sundays that my mother would tell me about her memories of her time overseas, of the wonderful ingredients she found there and what was, at the time, a burgeoning wine industry.

The inspiration closest to my heart is my brother. He was a trained chef when he was killed in a tragic accident at the age of 21, so when thinking about what I wanted to do, I felt compelled to follow in his footsteps. And in this way, we remained close, by sharing our mutual love for cooking and fresh, seasonal ingredients.

Like most chefs, I'm classically trained. My chef apprenticeship was completed at Restaurant Mignon in Blankenese. But the time I enjoyed the most was assisting my brother's friend's family run their small guesthouse in the Black Forest. Long before the terms 'kitchen garden' and 'foraging' entered common parlance, we grew all our own produce in the garden at the house, and I'd often spend time in the forest to see what herbs, berries and nuts we could pick and use.

Although I now live in a different country, I really enjoy drawing upon my German heritage and upbringing to cook the sort of food I came to love in Blankenese, this small, dreamy town, west of Hamburg. Many famous cities to the south of Hamburg, such as Munich, or to the east, such as Berlin, are landlocked and their cuisine is quite different with far less emphasis on seafood. The one unifying factor, however, in all the various regions of Germany, is beer. Every German loves a good beer and most regions in Germany have a local brewery!

Perhaps the link to the sea brought me eventually to settle in a beautiful beachside suburb with my family. My wife and I own a small, authentic German restuarant called Das Kaffeehaus. It is here that we share with the local community, the delight of German food cooked with love and from the heart.

Christopher Knuth

Soups

An aromatic, deep green soup — truly satisfying.

RAHMSPINATSUPPE

Cream of Spinach Soup

Remove stems from the spinach leaves and bring salted water to boil in a large pan. Add the spinach and cook for five to six minutes. Strain and reserve the liquid. Blend the spinach in a food processor or blender until pureed.

In a large pan, sauté the onions in the butter until pale golden brown. Remove from the heat and sprinkle in the flour and then return to the heat and a cook for another one to two minutes.

Stir in the liquid you reserved from the spinach and once it is all incorporated into the soup, bring it back to the boil. Cook until the texture is thick, then stir in the spinach puree and thickened cream.

Adjust the seasoning to your liking and serve the soup in bowls. Garnish with the eggs and crumbled bacon pieces.

570g (20oz) fresh young spinach, well washed
5 cups salted water
2 onions, finely chopped
2 tablespoons butter
3 tablespoons plain (all-purpose) flour
1 cup thickened cream
salt and pepper
2 hard-boiled eggs, sliced
2 strips crumbled bacon

This is a terrific soup. It's quite refreshing and makes the perfect starter or light lunch.

GURKEN–JOGHURT SUPPE MIT PINIENKERNE

Cucumber and Yoghurt Soup *with Pine Nuts*

Peel the cucumber and dice the flesh into small bite-size pieces and set aside.

Crush the garlic, pine nuts, salt and pepper thoroughly using a mortar and pestle. Transfer the mixture into a large bowl and beat in the yoghurt and diced cucumber. Add the water along with the lemon juice to taste.

Pour the soup into bowls to serve and scatter over a few pine nuts, drizzle with olive oil and garnish with some fresh dill.

1 large cucumber
4 garlic cloves
¾ cup pine nuts
½ teaspoon salt
pepper, to taste
400ml (13fl oz) natural yoghurt
120ml (4fl oz) cold water or chilled still mineral water
1–2 teaspoons lemon juice
½ cup pine nuts
1 teaspoon olive oil
dill

A quick meal for one, or a nourishing family dish for all times of the year.

Kürbissuppe mit Koriander

SERVES 6

Curried Sweet Potato, Coriander and *Pumpkin Soup*

1 butternut pumpkin, peeled and deseeded
2 large sweet potatoes
1 large onion
1 litre (33fl oz) vegetable or chicken stock
1 teaspoon ground coriander
1 teaspoon cumin
1 teaspoon garam masala
1 teaspoon turmeric
salt and pepper
coriander (cilantro) leaves
natural yoghurt or sour cream

Dice the pumpkin and sweet potatoes. Add to a large pot of boiling water and cook until soft.

Dice and sauté the onion in a frying pan with the ground coriander, cumin, garam masala and turmeric until soft, then add to the pot with the potatoes and puree well with a wand or hand blender and then simmer on low heat. Add salt and pepper to taste.

Chop fresh coriander and add liberally to the soup. Serve in bowls with a dollop of natural yoghurt or sour cream and a sprinkle of coriander.

This is a chunky and rustic soup and can be enjoyed perfectly with a glass of red wine and some crusty bread. A Knuth family favourite, it is a beautifully sustaining soup to warm the belly.

GULASCHSUPPE

Goulash Soup

1 tablespoon olive oil

400g (13oz) beef chuck steak, trimmed and cubed

1 medium brown onion, chopped

1 medium carrot, peeled and chopped

2 garlic cloves, crushed

1 teaspoon sweet paprika

3½ cups beef stock

400g (13oz) can diced tomatoes

450g (15oz) sebago potatoes, peeled, cubed

pepper, to taste

sour cream

fresh chives

Heat the oil in a saucepan over medium-high heat. Cook the steak, stirring constantly, in two batches, for two to three minutes or until browned. Transfer to a bowl.

Add the onion and carrot to the pan. Cook, stirring, for five minutes or until softened. Add the garlic and paprika. Cook, stirring, for 30 seconds or until fragrant. Stir in the stock and tomato.

Return the steak to the pan and bring to the boil. Reduce the heat to low, then simmer, covered, for one hour or until the steak is tender. Add the potatoes and cook, partially covered, for 30 minutes or until slightly thickened. Season with pepper.

Ladle into bowls, dollop with sour cream and sprinkle with chives, then serve.

A wonderfully hearty soup and a meal in itself.

GRAUPENSUPPE

German Barley Soup

Heat the butter in a very large saucepan over medium-high heat. Add the onion and cook, stirring, until soft, about five minutes. Add the barley, and cook, stirring, until lightly toasted, about five minutes. Add the stock, potato, carrot, celeriac, leek, marjoram, sausages and bacon, and cook, stirring occasionally, until sausages are tender, about 35 minutes.

Remove the sausages and bacon from the saucepan, and thinly slice the sausages. Discard the bacon.

Season the soup with the nutmeg, salt and pepper.

To serve, ladle the soup into serving bowls and garnish with parsley and the sliced sausage.

90g (3oz) unsalted butter
1 medium onion, finely chopped
1 cup pearl barley
2 litres (68fl oz) vegetable stock
½ cup russet potato, peeled and finely chopped
½ cup carrot, finely chopped
½ cup celeriac, finely chopped
½ cup leek, finely chopped
1 teaspoon dried marjoram
2 German sausages, bockwurst or bratwurst
60g (2oz) piece bacon
freshly grated nutmeg, to taste
salt and freshly ground black pepper, to taste
¹/₃ cup flat-leaf parsley leaves, thinly sliced

This classic soup is so delicious. It is also quick and easy to prepare.

ERBSEN-SCHINKENSUPPE

Ham and Green Pea Soup

Place ham or bacon bones in a large pot and cover with cold water. Add the soup mix, barley, and onion and simmer for one and a half hours.

Cook the peas and puree them. Remove the meat from the soup, pull the meat from the bone and add it add it back in to the soup. Add the potatoes and pureed green peas and thoroughly stir. Season with salt and pepper to taste and add the stock cube, if necessary. Simmer until the potato is soft.

Ladle into bowls and serve.

250g (8oz) ham or bacon bones
1 cup soup mix
½ cup barley
1 onion
2 cups frozen peas
2 potatoes
salt and pepper, to taste
1 vegetable stock cube

A very simple soup. This is comfort in a bowl.

Kartoffel-lauch-suppe mit Thymian

Leek, Potato and Thyme Soup

Dry the potato cubes on a paper towel.

Melt the butter in a saucepan and gradually add the leek and thyme. Sauté until golden, glazed and soft. This process generally takes about four to five minutes. Add the potato and enough water to cover the vegetables. Cover and cook on low heat for 30 minutes.

Pour in the milk and add salt and pepper and allow to simmer for a further 30 minutes.

Serve garnished with cream.

450g (14oz) potatoes, diced into
*   3cm (1in) cubes*
120g (4oz) butter
900g (1lb 13oz) leeks, washed and
*   trimmed*
1 large sprig of fresh thyme
300ml (10fl oz) full cream milk
salt and pepper
60ml (2fl oz) thickened cream

A nourishing soup just perfect to warm up your winter's evening.

LINSENSUPPE MIT SPECK

Lentil and Bacon Bockwurst Soup

1–2 teaspoons oil

1 onion, chopped

1 carrot, chopped

2 celery stalks, chopped

1 leek, chopped

1 parsnip, diced

400g (14oz) bacon, fat and rind
removed

2 bay leaves

1 cup brown lentils

8 cups water

3 bockwurst/bratwurst or kransky
sausage

salt and pepper to taste

continental parsley, chopped

bread, to serve

Heat the oil in a large saucepan and sauté the onion for five minutes until soft. Add the carrot, celery, leek, parsnip, bacon and bay leaves. Stir and gently sauté until golden brown.

Rinse the lentils thoroughly and add to the saucepan. Pour in the water and bring to the boil, turn down the heat, stir and simmer for about 40 to 50 minutes.

Cut the sausage into chunky pieces and add to the saucepan and simmer until tender.

Season with salt and pepper and garnish with parsley and serve with a slice of sourdough or rye bread.

You won't find an easier and tastier soup than this. The barley and chicken taste so good together. My Oma would make this for me when I was young and feeling unwell.

OMA'S HÜHNERSUPPE

SERVES 6

Grandma's Chicken Soup

750g (1½lbs) chicken pieces (thighs, drumsticks, wings)
salt and pepper
1 leek, diced
1 celery stalk
1 onion, chopped
1 garlic clove
1 stalk rosemary
8 cups water
200g (7oz) pearl barley
1 bay leaf
2 carrots, peeled and diced
½ cup cream, optional
garden herbs of your choice

Sauté the chicken in a large frying pan until golden brown. Remove from the pan and season.

Add the leek, celery, onion, garlic and rosemary to the pan and gently cook, stirring, for approximately six minutes until soft. Return the chicken pieces to the saucepan and pour in the water. Add the pearl barley, bay leaf and carrots then bring to the boil. Skim the surface and reduce to a simmer. Cook, partially covered, for one hour until the chicken and barley are tender.

Season and ladle into serving bowls and garnish with cream and fresh garden herbs.

A hearty classic, full of traditional German ingredients, this soup is as authentic as it is satisfying.

SERVES 4

SAUERKRAUT UND FLEISCHKLÖSCHEN SUPPE

Sauerkraut and Meatball Soup

Mix together the beef and the egg then season and form into meatballs.

Sauté the onions in the oil until translucent and add the sugar and continue to sauté until golden brown.

Add drained sauerkraut. Continue to sauté for a few minutes then add the paprika.

Pour in the beef broth and add the meatballs. Bring to the boil then simmer, covered, for about 15 minutes.

Add the potatoes and carrots and continue simmering for about 10 more minutes until the potatoes are tender.

Season with salt and pepper, if needed.

*500g (1lb) lean minced beef
    (ground beef)*
1 egg
salt and pepper
2 small onions, diced
60ml (2fl oz) oil
2 tablespoons sugar
*800g (28oz) canned sauerkraut,
    drained*
1 tablespoon paprika
4 cups beef broth (or bouillon)
*500g (1lb) potatoes, peeled and
    diced into 3cm (1in) pieces*
*2 or 3 carrots, peeled and diced into
    3cm (1in) pieces*

An unusual combination that tastes just delicous. And that red—magic!

ROTE BEETE SUPPE MIT WEISSKOHL

Cabbage and Beetroot Soup

Heat the oil in a large saucepan, add the onion and garlic, and cook gently for five minutes.

Mix in the beetroot, pour in the stock and boil until tender. Place in a blender, blend with the cider vinegar and then return to the saucepan.

Scatter the cabbage over the soup but don't stir. Cover and boil gently for five minutes, until the cabbage is almost cooked but still crunchy.

Serve with chives arranged on the top.

80ml (2½fl oz) grapeseed oil

1 onion, finely chopped

1 garlic clove, finely chopped

450g (15oz) raw baby beetroot, diced

1 litre (33fl oz) vegetable stock

2 tablespoons cider vinegar

275g (9oz) white cabbage, coarsely shredded

8 chive sprigs

Seafood

A great mid-week meal. Serve this with a fresh garden salad—no fuss and so quick to make.

THUNFISCH FRIKADELLEN

Tuna Fishcakes

500g (1 lb) potato
20g (¾oz) butter
2 tablespoons parsley, chopped
2 spring onions (scallions), chopped
coriander (cilantro), chopped
200g (7oz) tuna chunks
2 tablespoons plain (all-purpose)
　flour
salt and pepper
200g (7oz) breadcrumbs
oil

Boil the potatoes until soft, drain and mash with the butter.

Mix the parsley, spring onions, coriander, potatoes and tuna chunks together well.

Gradually add the flour and continue mixing until the mixture is well combined.

Season with salt and pepper.

Place the breadcrumbs in a bowl.

Form the tuna mix into 8 patties and toss them in the breadcrumbs to create a crispy outer layer.

Fry the patties in a frying pan with oil until golden brown on both sides.

Pickled herring is a popular fish in Germany—particularly Hamburg, where I spent many years as a child. As a seaport, Hamburg enjoys much produce fresh from the sea.

ROLLMOPS MIT KARTOFFEL UND TOMATENSALAT

SERVES 4

Pickled Herring *with Potato and Tomato Salad*

350g (11oz) new potatoes

4 rollmop herrings

110g (4oz) semi-dried tomatoes, chopped

80ml (2½fl oz) extra virgin-olive oil

Scrub the potatoes and place them in a saucepan of water. Bring to the boil and cook until tender. Leave to cool.

Unwrap the rollmops, keeping all the onion inside and place them on a plate.

Quarter the potatoes and mix in with the tomatoes. Drizzle with olive oil.

Serve potato and tomato mixture alongside the herrings.

This salad is stylish enough for entertaining, yet so simple to prepare. The delicious combination of citrus fruits is sure to please the tastebuds.

LACHSLEISTE MIT FRÜHKARTOFFELN UND ZITRUSFRUCHTSALAT

Seared Fillet of Salmon with New Potatoes and Citrus Salad

Boil the potatoes in salted water for approximately 12 to 15 minutes until just tender, then drain and allow them to cool a little before slicing. Season and drizzle over a little of the olive oil over the potatoes.

Drain the orange and lemon segments, reserving the juices, and remove to a separate bowl. Add 100ml (3fl oz) of the olive oil to the reserved juices and whisk together to combine, then season. Heat a non-stick frying pan and add the remaining olive oil. Season the salmon fillets and add to the pan, cooking them for about 3 to 4 minutes until seared and lightly golden. Flip over and cook for another minute until just tender.

Remove and place them on a plate to keep warm. Tip orange and lemon segments into the dressing and add the coriander and rocket leaves. Toss.

Arrange salmon fillets onto serving plates, placing the new potatoes on the side with the rocket salad on top.

16 small new potatoes, scrubbed clean
salt and pepper
125ml (4fl oz) olive oil
3 oranges, peeled and segmented
3 lemons, peeled and segmented
4 salmon fillets, skinned
1/3 cup coriander (cilantro), chopped
200g (7oz) rocket (arugula) leaves

Cod is abundant in the North Sea and this firm white-skinned fish is just perfect to serve with mustard sauce. It is featured in many German recipes and is also my father's favourite dish.

KABELJAU IN DER SENFSOßE

Cod *in Mustard Sauce*

Sprinkle the lemon juice over the cod fillets.

Combine the zest, onion, clove and bay leaf in a pan. Slowly pour in the water and bring to the boil, then reduce heat, cover and simmer for 20 minutes.

Add the cod fillets to the pan and cover and cook on low for 10 minutes.

To make the mustard sauce, ladle one cup of the cooking liquid into a saucepan and gently simmer until the liquid has reduced by half. Stir in the wholegrain mustard, add the butter and whisk until all the ingredients are well combined. Add in the parsley and season.

Place the cod fillets on a serving plate and pour over the mustard sauce. Garnish with a bay leaf or two and serve immediately, with boiled potatoes and asparagus.

juice and zest of 1 lemon
4 good-sized cod fillets
1 white onion
1 clove
1 bay leaf
5 cups water
¼ cup good quality wholegrain mustard
125g (4oz) butter
½ cup chopped continental parsley
salt and pepper
bay leaves

Salmon is a freshwater fish that has a good fresh taste. Perfect for marinating and grilling. Try this easy dish.

Marinierte Lachssteaks in Rotweinessig

Marinated Salmon Steaks in Red Wine Vinegar

4 salmon steaks
butter
2 tablespoons breadcrumbs
salt and pepper
2 tablespoons parsley

MARINADE
½ white onion, chopped
½ Spanish onion, chopped
3 cloves garlic, crushed
3 bay leaves
2 tablespoon mixed dried herbs
100ml (3fl oz) red wine vinegar
100ml (3fl oz) olive oil
salt and pepper

Combine the marinade in a bowl. Place the salmon in the marinade, cover and keep it in the marinade for approximately two hours.

Take the salmon out of the marinade and place on a buttered baking tray. Brush with melted butter, sprinkle with the dried breadcrumbs and season with salt and pepper.

Place under a pre-heated grill for five minutes until cooked. Garnish with parsley.

Serve with mashed potato or potato gratin and fresh garden salad with honey mustard dressing or cooked beans.

Hamburg is a seaport and I remember visiting the fish markets there, with my father, as a young child. Fish is traditionally a favourite dish in Hamburg. This goulash is a combination of a stew and a soup—great for a cold winter's night, served with rustic bread and butter.

FISCHGULASCH

Fish Goulash

2kg (4½lb) fresh mixed fish

2 white onions, chopped

4 cloves garlic, crushed

1 leek, chopped

3 teaspoons Hungarian paprika

salt, to taste

1 green pepper, seeded and sliced
   lengthways

1 red pepper, seeded and sliced
   lengthways

good quality tomatoes

2 stalks celery, chopped

½ cup white wine (preferably Riesling)

sour cream

parsley

Skin and fillet the fish, refrigerate the fillets, then place all the bones, fish heads and skin into a large pan along with the onions, garlic, leek, paprika and salt. Cover with water and bring to the boil then reduce the heat and simmer for one to one and a half hours. Strain the stock thoroughly.

In a separate frying pan, add the fish fillets, red and green peppers, tomatoes and celery, and slowly add the fish stock. Cook gently on low heat, gradually adding the wine as it simmers. Cook for approximately 10 to 12 minutes.

Season to taste with salt and pepper, pour in to warm bowls, garnish with a dollop of sour cream and fresh chopped parsley and serve immediately with sourdough or linseed bread.

Blaue Forelle *is a German speciality, served on a bed of sauerkraut and caraway seeds and garnished with fresh bay leaves and lemon slices. This visually stunning dish is sure to delight guests at your next dinner party.*

SERVES 4

BLAUE FORELLE MIT WEISSWEINESSIG UND PORREE

Oven-baked Blue Trout *with White Wine Vinegar and Leek*

Pre-heat the oven to 180°C (350°F/Gas Mark 4).

Rub the skin of the trout with the sea salt and place in a roasting pan.

In a saucepan bring the white wine vinegar to the boil and slowly pour this over the trout.

Rapidly cool the fish by fanning the pan or let it stand in a draft for five minutes.

Bring the pan back to the boil and add the leeks, bay leaves, and peppercorns. Cover the roasting pan with aluminium foil and bake for about 30 minutes or until the fish is cooked.

Transfer the trout to individual plates and serve on a bed of sauerkraut with fresh bay leaves and lemon to garnish.

4 trout (around 185g/6oz each)
3 teaspoons sea salt
2 ½ cups white wine vinegar
2 leeks, sliced
2 bay leaves
8 whole black peppercorn
sauerkraut
bay leaves and lemon slices
½ cup melted butter

You can never go wrong when serving smoked salmon. It goes wonderfully with potatoes, lemon and dill. Serve warm with rye bread.

SERVES 4

GERÄUCHERTER LACHS UND WARMER KARTOFFELSALAT MIT ZITRONENDILL DRESSING

Smoked Salmon *and Warm Potato Salad*
Served with Lemon Dill Dressing

Boil, steam or microwave the chat potatoes until cooked, then cover and keep warm.

Combine all the dressing ingredients in a large bowl then add in the potatoes. Gently mix in the salmon and season to taste.

Fill the iceberg lettuce cups with the potato salad and serve.

400g (13oz) baby chat potatoes
  quartered
400g (13oz) smoked salmon slices
4 iceberg lettuce cups

LEMON AND DILL DRESSING
2 tablespoons dill, finely chopped
90ml (2½fl oz) lemon juice
1 tablespoon olive oil
1 garlic clove, crushed
100g (3½oz) yoghurt

This dish is light and fresh. Served with a fresh garden salad it's great as a starter or light lunch. Enjoy with a chilled glass of pinot gris.

SAUTIERTE GARNELE MIT GRÜNER SOSSE

Sautéed Prawns (Shrimp) *with Green Sauce*

1 kg (2lbs) fresh uncooked prawns
  (shrimp)
80ml (2½fl oz) olive oil
rocket (arugula)

GREEN SAUCE
1 clove garlic, peeled
salt and pepper, to taste
1 bunch flat leaf parsley, washed
  and dried
1 bunch basil, washed and dried
1 bunch chives, washed and dried
rosemary
½ teaspoon turmeric
mint, washed and dried
1 spring onion
80ml (2½fl oz) olive oil
juice of ½ a lemon

To prepare the sauce, combine all the ingredients except the oil and juice in a blender. Pour in two to three tablespoons of the olive oil and the lemon juice, blend and then add in an extra two to three tablespoons of water and the rest of the olive oil. Refrigerate in covered bowl for at least one hour before serving with the prawns (shrimp).

Sauté the fresh prawns (shrimp) in the oil on a high heat in a pan for three to four minutes until they have changed colour but are still soft and fleshy to touch. Take them off the heat and let them cool slightly.

Arrange the prawns (shrimp) on individual serving plates on a bed of fresh rocket with sauce on the side.

A really impressive dish great for dinner parties. This is a superb seafood dish that tastes great too.

SCHOLLE MIT HEISSER DILLSENFSOßE

Flounder *with Hot Dill Mustard Sauce*

olive oil

4 medium flounder, washed and
  dried

½ bunch dill, finely chopped

2 lemons, sliced into wedges

HOT DILL MUSTARD SAUCE

35g (1¼oz) butter

40g (1½oz) flour

500ml (16fl oz) fish stock

60ml (2fl oz) hot mustard

2 egg yolks

salt and white pepper

pinch of sugar

1 tablespoon white wine vinegar

1 tablespoon lemon juice

To prepare the sauce, fry the butter and flour in a pan until golden in colour.

Add the fish stock whilst stirring and slowly simmer for 15 to 20 minutes, stirring occasionally. Mix the mustard, egg yolks, salt and pepper, sugar, white wine vinegar, and lemon juice together. Take the sauce off the heat and slowly add the mustard mixture to it, gently combining all the ingredients together.

Pre-heat a large frying pan and brush with the olive oil. Add the flounder to the pan and brush each side with a little of the olive oil. Cook for three to four minutes or until cooked through.

Arrange four plates and transfer a flounder to each plate. Pour the sauce over the flounder and garnish with fresh dill and lemon wedges.

Accompany this with sautéed baby herb chat potatoes and seasonal greens.

Meat, Game
&
Poultry

The schnitzel is a traditional dish of the homeland and my personal favourite.

SERVES 4

HUHN SCHNITZEL

Chicken Schnitzel

Wash the chicken breasts, pat dry with paper towel and place on a clean chopping board.

Trim off unwanted fat and membrane then butterfly each chicken breast by positioning so that its tip is facing you. Place your non-cutting hand on top of the breast. Insert your knife into the thickest part of the breast and slice into the breast until the knife reaches the middle. Make sure that the knife is cutting through two equal thicknesses of the breast. Open it like a book.

Place into a fridge to cool and rest the meat.

Use a mallet to flatten the chicken breast.

Prepare three flat and wide trays. Place plain flour in one, beaten egg in the second tray and breadcrumbs in the third.

Dip the breasts into the flour, shake off excess, then dip into the egg and then the crumbs.

Fry in the oil until brown all over and cooked through.

4 chicken breasts
1 egg
½ cup plain (all-purpose) flour
2 cups good quality breadcrumbs
vegetable oil

Rustic, tasty and tender, a delicious German favourite.

RINDFLEISCH ROULADEN

SERVES 4 – 6

Beef Rouladen

*500g (1 lb) round steak 1cm (½in)
   thick*
salt and pepper
60ml (2fl oz) Dijon mustard
6 slices prosciutto
1 red onion, chopped
½ cup dill pickle, chopped
2 cups flour
olive oil
200ml (7fl oz) beef stock
100ml (3fl oz) red wine
1 cup water
2 rosemary sprigs
flour or cornflour (cornstarch)
2 tablespoons sour cream or yoghurt
curly parsley

Cut the steak into pieces, 5 x 10cm (2 x 4in) then pound until the steak is very thin.

Season strips with salt and pepper and spread a thin layer of Dijon mustard on one side.

Chop prosciutto into small pieces. Place one tablespoon of red onion, one tablespoon of prosciutto pieces and one tablespoon of dill pickle in the middle of each steak. Roll the steak up and thread a toothpick into the meat to hold steak roll together. Repeat until all meat is rolled.

Place flour into a mixing bowl and coat individual rouladen on all sides.

In a large frying pan or baking pot, cook the rolls in olive oil. Add the beef stock, red wine and water to a depth of half an inch. Add the rosemary sprigs. Cover the pan and simmer adding further water and beef stock as needed to keep the meat covered. Turn rouladen from time to time in the sauce. Cook on low heat for about one hour or until roulade are tender. Remove to a heated serving dish.

Pre-heat oven to 160°C (325°F/Gas Mark 3).

Thicken the gravy with a little flour or cornflour. Add sour cream or yoghurt then pour over the rouladen and place in the oven for a further 5 to 10 minutes.

Garnish with curly parsley and serve with mashed potatoes, spätzel or noodles and honey-glazed carrots.

VARIATIONS ON ROULADEN STUFFING

§ prosciutto, Swiss cheese and spinach

§ smoked ham, gruyere cheese and wholegrain mustard

§ red pepper, bacon, spinach and tasty cheese

A traditional German meat dish that originates from the south of Germany—an authentic dish.

DEUTSCHE ROULADEN

German Rouladen

Cut the flank steak into thin fillets, about 10cm (4in) thick and 8cm (3in) wide. Generously spread one side of each fillet with mustard.

Place bacon, onions and pickle slices on each fillet and form into a roll. Use string or toothpicks to hold the roll together.

Heat a frying pan over medium heat and melt the butter. Place the rolls in the butter and sauté until browned.

Pour in two and a half cups of water and the bouillon cube, stirring to dissolve. Simmer for about one hour.

750g (1½lb) flank steak
1½ tablespoons Dijon or wholegrain mustard
250g (½lb) thick sliced bacon
2 large onions, sliced
dill or garlic pickle slices
2 tablespoons butter
2½ cups water
1 cube beef bouillon

Schmor is 'braised' and brata is 'roasted' in German. A great winter dish—beef and beer go together here like magic.

RINDFLEISCH SCHMORBRATEN GESCHMORT IN DUNKEL WEISS BEIR

SERVES 4–6

Beef Pot Roast *Braised in Dark Lager Beer*

1½kg (3lb) chuck roast
salt and pepper
olive oil
1 can dark beer
2 tablespoons paprika
1 teaspoon garlic, crushed
2 bay leaves
12 peppercorns
1 red capsicum (bell pepper), chopped
1 green capsicum (bell pepper), chopped
1½kg (3lb) baby chat potatoes
2 large onions, quartered

Season the roast and brown in a large frying pan with olive oil.

In a slow cooker or crock pot, pour in a little dark beer at the bottom of the pot before placing the roast inside. Pour in the remainder of the dark beer then add the paprika, garlic, bay leaves, peppercorns and capsicum and turn the slowcooker to high. Add the whole baby chats and onion and cook for three to six hours until the meat falls easily from a fork.

Serve with fresh sauerkraut or red cabbage on the side.

This is an exellent dish that has a great texture.

Huhn mit Walnuss Salat

Chicken and Walnut Salad

500g (1 lb) cooked chicken meat,
   chopped
2 celery sticks, coarsely chopped
1 large apple, cored and diced
½ cup of walnuts, roughly chopped
⅓ cup mayonnaise
1–2 tablespoons cream, optional
watercress sprigs

Place the chicken in a large bowl with the celery, apple and walnuts. Thin the mayonnaise if necessary by adding a small amount of cream to give the consistency of thick cream.

Pour over the chicken and toss well until the ingredients are evenly coated. Turn into a serving dish and garnish with watercress.

Serve this with garlic mashed potatoes and green beans. This is seriously tasty.

Hühnerbrust mit Sahniger Pilz-soße

Chicken Breast *and Creamy Mushroom Sauce*

Divide each chicken breast into two fillets, place them between two sheets of cling wrap and flatten with a rolling pin to a thickness of 1cm (½in). Cut into 2½cm (1in) strips diagonally across the fillets.

Heat 2 tablespoons of the oil in a frying pan and cook the onion slowly until soft but not browned. Add the mushrooms and cook until golden brown. Remove from the pan and keep warm.

Increase the heat, add the remaining oil and fry the chicken quickly, in small batches, for about 3 to 4 minutes until lightly coloured. Return the onions and mushrooms to the pan and season with the salt and black pepper. Stir in the sour cream and bring to the boil. Sprinkle with fresh tarragon and serve.

4 large chicken breasts
45ml (1½fl oz) olive oil
1 large onion, thinly sliced
3 cups mushrooms, sliced
salt and black pepper
1¼ cups sour cream
1 tablespoon fresh tarragon, chopped

The mustard in this dish gives the sauce an edge. The sauce simply transforms the chicken breast into a delectable meal.

HÜHNERBRUST IN SENF-SALBEI-SOßE

Chicken Breast *with Creamy Mustard and Sage Sauce*

Cut the chicken into strips, then heat the oil and butter in the pan and sauté the chicken over medium heat until lightly golden.

In a saucepan, heat the stock and the cream, stir in the Dijon and wholegrain seeded mustard and the sage. Squeeze in the juice if using.

Serve with fresh green beans and mash.

500g (1 lb) chicken breast
1 teaspoon oil
1 teaspoon butter
chicken stock
250ml (8 fl oz) cream
1 tablespoon Dijon mustard
3 tablespoons wholegrain mustard
1 tablespoon freshly chopped sage
juice of ½ lemon or lime, optional

Great with mashed potato or pasta this is a good family meal—quick and easy to make, it will warm you from the inside out.

HUHNSTROGANOFF

Chicken Stroganoff

4 large chicken breasts
60ml (2fl oz) olive oil
1 large onion, thinly sliced
3 cups mushrooms, sliced
salt and black pepper
1¼ cups sour cream
1 tablespoon fresh parsley, chopped

Divide each chicken breast into two fillets, place them between two sheets of cling wrap and flatten with a rolling pin to a thickness of 1cm (½in). Cut into 2½cm (1in) strips diagonally across the fillets.

Heat 2 tablespoons of the oil in a frying pan and cook the onion slowly until soft but not browned. Add the mushrooms and cook until golden brown. Remove from the pan and keep warm.

Increase the heat, add the remaining oil and fry the chicken quickly, in small batches, for about 3 to 4 minutes until lightly coloured. Return the onions and mushrooms to the pan and season with the salt and black pepper. Stir in the sour cream and bring to the boil. Sprinkle with fresh parsley and serve.

SELBST GEMACHTE HÜHNERBRÜHE

Homemade Chicken Stock

Fill a large pot with the water and add the chicken pieces. Bring to the boil then reduce the heat to simmer, skimming any fat from the surface.

Add the onion, celery, leek, bay leaves and seasoning and simmer over low heat for 2 hours.

Strain the stock into a large bowl and allow to cool then refrigerate or freeze in portions

1 free-range chicken, cut into pieces
3 litres (100fl oz) water
1 onion
2 celery sticks
1 leek
2 bay leaves
freshly ground pepper, to taste

This dish is sure to please and easy to make. Honey and mustard are ingredients found in most household pantries. Serve with boiled pototoes and diced carrots for an authentic meal.

SERVES 4

HONIGSENFHUHN

Honey Mustard Chicken

Place the chicken in a bowl with the olive oil, lemon juice, salt and pepper, mustard and honey. Marinate in the fridge for one hour.

Fry the onion and zest in a large pan until the onion is soft. Add the chicken and cook on both sides until golden. Pour in the stock and wine, add the bay leaf then slowly bring to the boil and then simmer slowly for 20 minutes. Season to taste.

Garnish with flat-leaf parsley and serve with boiled baby potatoes and diced carrots.

8 chicken thighs
olive oil
juice and zest of 1 lemon
salt and pepper, to taste
2 teaspoons wholegrain mustard
1 tablespoon honey
1 onion
1 litre (33fl oz) chicken stock
250ml (8fl oz) white wine
1 bay leaf
¼ cup flat-leaf parsley

A zesty dish with fantastic aromas. Low in fat and simple to prepare.

ORANGE-HONIG HUHN

Orange, Thyme and Honey Chicken

4 chicken breasts
oil
juice and zest of 3 oranges
3 teaspoons honey
1 teaspoon fresh thyme
1 teaspoon olive oil
salt and pepper

Sauté the chicken in a pan with the oil until golden on both sides.

In a bowl, combine the juice, zest, honey and thyme.

Pour mixture into the pan over the chicken and simmer for a further ten minutes or until the chicken is cooked through.

Serve with baked chat potatoes and a fresh apple and pear salad.

Serve with a crisp green salad and baby chat potatoes. Or try this with spätzle, a traditional German noodle. Delicious authentic cuisine.

SPECK, SAUERKRAUT UND TOMATEN HUHN

Simmered Bacon, Sauerkraut and Tomato Chicken

1 teaspoon olive oil

4 rashers bacon, diced

1 large white onion, diced

2 cloves garlic

2 x 400g (13oz) cans diced tomato

1 tablespoon tomato puree

250g (8oz) sauerkraut

4 chicken breasts

½ cup white wine (preferably Riesling)

fresh curly parsley

Sauté the diced onion and bacon in the oil over high heat until the bacon starts to colour. Add the garlic and continue to cook for a further two minutes or until the onion is soft.

Add the chicken and cook for two minutes each side until golden brown. Add the canned tomato, tomato puree and sauerkraut. Pour in the white wine, stir and cook for a further 8 minutes.

Season to taste then simmer over low heat for a further ten minutes.

Garnish with fresh parsley and serve with spätzle or noodle.

This dish is particularly good if served with hot potatoes in their jackets and sour cream or with French bread.

SERVES 10

Eingelegtes Schweinefleisch

Mulled Pork

Place all the ingredients in a large pan or ideally in a crockpot and place it in the fridge overnight. If cooking the same evening leave as long as possible. (Crock pots can be set on low before going to work or high if cooking that evening.)

If using a good old-fashioned pot, set it on the heat, bring to the boil and simmer gently for 40 to 60 minutes.

When the meat is tender, check seasonings and consistency; if it is too liquid, remove the lid and reduce by turning up the heat or mix in a little arrowroot dissolved in water and stir in.

1 kg (2 lb) pork shoulder or foreloin, diced
750 ml (24 fl oz) red wine
2½ tablespoons brandy
juice and zest of 2 oranges
juice and zest of 1 lemon
1 tablespoon soft brown sugar
6 cloves
6 juniper berries
½ cup sultanas
1 tablespoon beef stock powder
4 apples, sliced
3 onions, sliced
4 cloves garlic, crushed
2 teaspoons cinnamon
2 teaspoons nutmeg
salt and pepper, to taste

Deliciously indulgent and mouth-watering.

Schweinekoteletts in Senfsoße

Pork Chops *with Mustard Sauce*

Melt the butter in a frying pan, add the onion and sauté until soft. Remove from the pan and set aside.

Coat the chops with the flour that has been seasoned with salt and pepper, add them to the pan and fry both sides until golden brown.

Return the onion to the pan and pour in the sherry and chicken stock. Cover and simmer on low heat for 30 minutes or until the chops are cooked.

Stir in the mustard, season to taste and garnish with fresh rosemary.

30g (1oz) butter
1 onion, finely chopped
4 pork chops
1 tablespoon flour
salt and pepper
½ cup medium sherry
190ml (6fl oz) chicken stock
2 tablespoons light Dijon mustard
fresh rosemary

A fantastic and appealing dish. The freshly stewed plums marry beautifully with the pork. Serve with seasonal vegetables.

SCHWEINEFLEISCHLEISTE MIT GEDÄMPFTEN PFLAUMEN

Pork Fillet *with Freshly Stewed Plums*

Pre-heat the oven to 180°C (350°F/Gas Mark 4). Season the flour with salt and pepper and use to coat the pork.

Melt the butter in a frying pan, add the pork and fry until golden brown on both sides. Transfer to a casserole dish.

Mash the plums to a coarse puree, stir in the cinnamon and wine then pour over the pork.

Cover and cook in the oven for 30 minutes then serve hot, garnished with the parsley.

2 tablespoons plain (all-purpose) flour
salt and pepper
500g (1 lb) pork fillet, cut into 4 pieces
60g (2oz) butter
1 x 425g (14oz) can purple plums, drained and stoned
¼ teaspoon ground cinnamon
160ml (5fl oz) red wine
parsley, chopped

Another simple and delicious meal—homestyle cooking at its best. Sage and cider pair perfectly with the pork. Serve this dish straight from the casserole dish at the table.

SALBEI-SCHWEINEFLEISCH IN APFELWEIN

SERVES 10

Sage Pork *in Cider*

100g (3½oz) butter

2 large onions, sliced

4 apples, sliced

¼ cup arrowroot

2 teaspoons beef stock powder

1kg (2lb) pork shoulder or foreloin, diced

750ml (24fl oz) bottle dry cider

2 teaspoons sugar

¼ cup apple concentrate

1½ tablespoons fresh sage, chopped, or 1 tablespoon dried

salt and pepper, to taste

dash of calvados

Melt half the butter in a large frying pan and fry the onion until soft. Add the apples and continue cooking gently for a further five to ten minutes. Transfer to a casserole or crockpot.

Combine the arrowroot and stock powder and use it to coat the pork then heat the remaining butter and brown the pork, sealing the edges.

Add the diced pork, apple concentrate and sage to the pot and simmer for approximately 40 minutes. Once the meat is tender, add the salt and pepper and more sage if desired and a dash of calvados.

This dish is a favourite of my father's. Serve over a bed of mash with plenty of sauce.

OMA'S PAPRIKA SCHWEINEKOTTLETTS

Grandma's Paprika Pork Cutlets

4 x 180g (6oz) pork cutlets
salt
60ml (2fl oz/ ¼ cup) oil
100g (3fl oz) bacon or speck, diced
1 white onion
2 tablespoons tomato paste
4 green capsicums (peppers), thinly
   sliced
1 tablespoon mild paprika
200g (7oz) sour cream
fresh parsley

Place pork cutlets on a chopping board and lightly salt.

Add the oil to a frying pan and cook the cutlets on medium heat until cooked through. Remove from the pan and set aside.

Add diced bacon or speck and the onion to the pan. Sauté until the bacon is slightly golden and the onion is soft. Add the tomato paste, capsicums and paprika, stir and lower the heat to a simmer, then stir in the sour cream and mix well.

Place the cutlets back in the pan and cook on low heat for a further 10 minutes.

Arrange the cutlets on a plate over a bed of mashed potato and pour over the sauce and garnish with fresh parsley.

Serve immediately with a side of red cabbage or seasonal greens.

A great combination of traditional German fare and a sustaining and warming dish that wakes the tastebuds.

SCHWEINEFLEISCH MIT SAUERKRAUT

Pork Stew *with Sauerkraut*

Heat the oil in a large pan and brown the onion and crushed garlic cloves until soft

Add the pork cubes to the pan and fry until browned. Stir in the caraway seeds and fresh dill, and pour in the stock. Cook for 1 hour over low heat.

Stir the drained sauerkraut into the pork with the paprika. Let it simmer for 45 minutes. Add salt to taste.

Garnish the stew with a little more dill and serve with sour cream, sprinkled with paprika.

2 tablespoons vegetable oil

2 onions, finely chopped

2 garlic cloves, crushed

1 kg (2lb) lean pork, cut into 5cm (2in) cubes

1 teaspoon caraway seeds

2 tablespoons fresh dill, chopped

3¾ cups warm pork or vegetable stock

4 cups sauerkraut, drained

1 tablespoon paprika, plus extra to serve

salt

sour cream

KALBFLEISCHBRATEN

Veal Roast

Pre-heat the oven to 180°C (350°F/Gas Mark 4).

Place the veal or pork between two pieces of cling wrap and pound with a rolling pin or mallet to flatten into a regular shape. Season well.

Top each slice with a layer of bacon and ham. Beat the eggs in a small pan with the milk and stir over a low heat until softly scrambled. Let cool.

Layer the scrambled eggs on top of each slice and spread with a knife, then sprinkle on the pickles. Roll up each slice carefully. Tie the rolls securely at intervals with string.

On the stove, melt butter in a large casserole dish. Add the meat rolls and brown all over. Remove the pan from the heat and put the rolls on to a plate. Spread the flour into the pan and stir thoroughly. Put the pan back on heat and cook flour mixture until light brown, then slowly add half of the water or stock. Return the meat rolls to the pan and bring to a boil, then place casserole in the oven for 1¾ to 2 hours to roast slowly, adding in the remaining water during cooking if necessary to stop the meat drying out.

When cooked, let the rolls cool for ten minutes before slicing. Serve with gravy and baby carrots, green beans and dill pickles.

1.3kg (3lb) shoulder of veal or lean pork, cut into 1½cm slices
salt and freshly ground black pepper
230g (7½oz) bacon
170g (5½oz) sliced ham
4 beaten eggs
60ml (2fl oz) milk
3 dill pickles, finely diced
125g (4oz) butter
¼ cup self-raising (self-rising) flour
375ml (12floz/1½ cups) water or chicken stock

Creamy and delicious, this is a real favourite of mine. Serve with spätzle, or plain white rice. This is a perfect, cosy dinner party option as it can be prepared in advance.

SERVES 4

OMA'S KALBFLEISCHSTROGANOFF

Grandma's Veal Stroganoff

Pound the schnitzel until soft then cut into thin strips.

Melt half the butter in a frying pan over low heat. Add the onion and the whole mushroom caps and stir in the tomato paste and flour. Stir over low heat for two to three minutes, then set aside.

In a clean frying pan, heat the remaining butter and add veal and fry over high heat, turning until evenly browned. Lower the heat, add the sauce to the pan followed by the sour cream, salt and pepper, lemon juice and splash of wine then return to medium heat. Gently stir.

Garnish with fresh watercress and serve immediately with noodles or plain white rice.

4 veal schnitzels

60g (2oz) butter

1 large white onion, diced

250g (8oz) button mushrooms, stalks removed

2 tablespoons tomato paste

1 tablespoon plain (all-purpose) flour

½ cup sour cream

salt and pepper

2 tablespoons lemon juice

splash of port or red wine, to taste

1 bunch watercress

Just delicious! Veal schnitzel is a breaded veal cutlet often served with fresh parsley and a lemon wedge. You can vary this dish by adding a mushroom sauce, or a tomato-based spicy capsicum sauce.

KALBFLEISCH SCHNITZEL

SERVES 4

Veal Schnitzel

4 veal cutlets, thinly sliced
salt and pepper
1 egg
½ cup plain (all-purpose) flour
2 cups good quality breadcrumbs
vegetable oil

Place the veal between two pieces of cling wrap and pound with a rolling pin or mallet to flatten to ½cm (¼in). Season well.

Pound the veal cutlet with a mallet until quarter of an inch thick and set aside. The pounding helps to tenderise the meat

Prepare three flat and wide trays. Place plain flour in one, beaten egg in the second tray and breadcrumbs in the third.

Dip the veal into the flour, shake off any excess, then dip into the egg and then the crumbs, pressing gently into the breadcrumbs to ensure they are well coated.

Heat the frying pan with oil and place the veal into the pan, there should be enough oil to ensure it swims in it.

Fry over medium heat on both sides until golden brown. For the perfect schnitzel the oil should be hot enough to brown it in 3 minutes and the coat crisp and brown.

Serve immediately.

Meat Loaf is such a wonderful comfort food. I remember my mother making this on many a cold winter's day. It goes nicely with a good quality relish or chutney. It can also be sliced and eaten with freshly cut bread and salad.

FALSCHER HASE

Meat Loaf

1 tablespoon oil

3 bacon rashers, finely chopped

2 cloves garlic, diced

½ brown onion, diced

½ red onion, diced

5 slices bread

¾ cup milk

1 kg (2lb) lean mince

2 free-range eggs

50g (2oz) tomato paste

salt and pepper

continental parsley, finely chopped

Pre-heat oven to 180°C (350°F/Gas Mark 4).

Heat the oil in a frying pan, add the bacon, the garlic and the brown and red onion. Sauté until the onion is soft then set aside to cool.

Cut the bread into cubes, add to a bowl and pour milk over it. Leave to soak until the milk is absorbed by the bread.

Combine the onion and bacon mixture, the bread mixture, the mince, eggs, tomato paste and salt and pepper in a large bowl and mix well, then add the parsley.

Oil a loaf pan well and spoon the meatloaf mixture into it. Bake for 50 to 60 minutes or until cooked through. Let it stand to cool for five to ten minutes before slicing.

Garnish freely with fresh continental parsley and serve immediately with fresh seasonal vegetables or fresh garden salad with relish and chutney on the side.

This is a delightful dish—great for that special event to be celebrated in style. Surround the duck with baked potatoes, onions and carrots.

SERVES 4–6

GEFÜLLTE ENTE MIT SAUERKRAUT UND APFEL

Duck *with Sauerkraut and Apple Stuffing*

Pre-heat the oven to moderate, 180°C (350°F/Gas Mark 4).

In a frying pan, heat the oil and sauté the onion until transparent, add the apples and cook until golden.

Stir in the brown sugar, salt and freshly ground pepper, half the thyme and the caraway seeds, then add the sauerkraut to the pan and toss through the mixture over medium heat.

Leave to cool.

Prepare the duck by wiping the skin inside and out with a damp cloth or absorbent paper. Rub the duck with the remaining olive oil and season with salt and pepper.

Stuff the duck with the sauerkraut and apple mixture. Truss the duck, prick well with a fork and place on a rack in a roasting pan. Roast for two to two and a half hours, remembering to prick the skin and baste every 30 minutes to allow the fat to escape.

Serve on a platter garnished with watercress and fresh apple slices.

2 tablespoons olive oil

1 large Spanish onion, coarsely chopped

2 cooking apples, peeled, cored and diced

2 tablespoons brown sugar

salt and freshly ground pepper

fresh bunch thyme

1 teaspoon caraway seeds

700g (24oz) sauerkraut

1.8–2.3kg (4–5lb) duck

watercress

1 apple, sliced

Beautiful served with roasted baby chat potatoes and red cabbage.

LAMMSTEAK IN APRIKOSENSOßE

Lamb Steaks *with Fresh Apricot Sauce*

To make the sauce, pour the nectar into a shallow frying pan and bring to the boil. Add the dried apricots, honey, mint and lemon zest and juice. Simmer on low for 20 minutes, stirring occasionally.

Heat the grill to high. Mix the honey with the oil and lightly brush over the steaks. Season with salt and pepper. Grill on high heat for four to five minutes each side for medium rare. If you prefer well-done, grill for a few more minutes.

Garnish each steak with a sprig of mint and serve on a pool of sauce.

2 tablespoons honey
2 tablespoons olive oil
150g (5oz) lamb steaks
salt and ground black pepper

APRICOT SAUCE
400ml (13fl oz) can apricot nectar
½ cup dried apricots
2 tablespoons honey
2 tablespoons chopped mint
few drops lemon juice
½ teaspoon grated lemon zest
1 tablespoon lemon juice

Nürnberger is an authentic German sausage from Nurnberg. It is a relatively small pork sausage (about 8cm/3¼in). You'll find street stands in Nurberg that sell this in a bread roll, often served with sauerkraut. You can find these sausages in any good German butcher or delicatessen.

SERVES 4

GESCHMORTE NÜRNBERGER MIT LINSEN

Nurnberg Sausage *and Lentil Braise*

Pre-heat the oven to 180°C (350°F/Gas Mark 4).

Sauté the carrots and parsnips in a tablespoon of the olive oil, then place in a baking tray and season with salt and pepper, thyme and rosemary. Roast the vegetables in the oven for approximately 25 minutes, turning once until golden and cooked through.

While the vegetables are roasting, sauté the sausages in the frying pan until golden and then set aside.

Drain the oil from the pan, leaving only one tablespoon to sauté the remaining ingredients. Sauté the onion over low heat for approximately 20 minutes until soft and tender. Add in the garlic, brown sugar, balsamic vinegar and the remaining two tablespoons of thyme and rosemary then cook. Stir in the beef stock, red wine and lentils and cook for a further five to ten minutes then serve garnished with whole flat-leaf parsley.

1 bunch Dutch carrots, peeled

2 parsnips, peeled and cut lengthways

60ml (2fl oz) olive oil

salt and pepper

¼ cup chopped thyme leaves

¼ cup rosemary

10 Nürnberger sausages

2 onions

2 garlic cloves, crushed

1 teaspoon brown sugar

2 tablespoons balsamic vinegar

2½ tablespoons red wine

250ml (8fl oz/1 cup) beef stock

1 can brown lentils, rinsed and drained

3 teaspoons fresh flat-leaf parsley

This can easily be frozen but only add the sour cream after it has been defrosted and warmed up. Great with noodles or rice or even as a baked potato filling.

HACKFLEISCHAUFLAUF

German Minced Meat Casserole

2 onions, diced

1 tablespoon oil

1 tablespoon butter

500g (1 lb) minced beef (ground beef)

1 leek, sliced

5 tablespoons tomato paste

250ml (8fl oz) stock

1 tablespoon mustard

1 teaspoon mild paprika

1 teaspoon salt

¼ cup sour cream

Fry the diced onion in the oil and butter in a casserole dish over a low heat. Then turn up the heat and add the mince, stirring it until it is brown.

Add the leek, tomato paste, stock, mustard and paprika and season to taste.

Let it simmer for about 15 minutes. Add the sour cream shortly before serving.

This simple, yet tasty, meal is a great mid-week meal.

EIERPFANNKUCHEN MIT SPECK

Egg Cakes *with Bacon*

125g (4oz) bacon, sliced
4 eggs
1 tablespoon flour
80ml (2½fl oz) milk
 salt and ground pepper
1 bunch chives, chopped

Fry the bacon then remove from the pan and keep warm. Pour half of the bacon fat out of the pan.

Mix the eggs with the flour, milk, salt and pepper.

Heat up the remaining bacon fat in the pan and pour in the egg mixture and leave it to cook. Lay the bacon slices on top of it. Briefly place the pan under the grill to brown the top.

To serve, sprinkle with chives and serve with salad and bread or bread rolls.

This recipe is from my grandmother and was a favourite of my father when he was a child. Great served with potatoes.

EIER IN SENFSOßE

Eggs *in Mustard Sauce*

Melt the butter in a pan over a medium heat and then add the flour. Stir continuously until golden in colour. Be careful not to let the flour burn as this will make the sauce bitter.

Gradually add the stock, a little at a time, stirring continuously. Mix in the sour cream and mustard, stirring until smooth. Bring the sauce to the boil and then let it simmer for 10 minutes. Add the salt, pepper, sugar and nutmeg to taste, then stir in the chives.

Wash the chives and then chop them up adding them to the sauce.

Boil the eggs for 6 to 8 minutes, take them out, plunge them into cold water and then peel them and put them into the sauce.

40g (1½oz) butter or margarine
½ cup flour
250ml (9fl oz) vegetable stock, warm
250g (8oz) sour cream
3 tablespoons mustard
salt and pepper
nutmeg
pinch of sugar
1 bunch chives, chopped
8 eggs

These go particularly well with potatoes and parsley or rice.

GEFÜLLTE PAPRIKASCHOTEN

Stuffed Capsicums

Pre-heat oven to 200°C (400°F/Gas Mark 5).

Cut a third lengthwise off each capsicum, getting rid of the pips and internal membrane. Finely slice the remaining capsicum.

Mix together half of the marjoram, mince, egg, chives, paprika, tomato paste and one tablespoon of the sour cream. Season.

Fill the peppers with the mixture, adding the remaining marjoram.

Place the peppers in a casserole dish, drizzle the oil over them and add the stock to the dish. Bake for 50 minutes.

Remove the dish from oven, spoon out the sauce and mix it in with the sauce thickener over a low heat. Add the rest of the sour cream and salt and pepper.

Serve the capsicums with the sauce.

4 medium sized capsicums (bell peppers)
6 stalks of marjoram
300g (10z) minced beef (ground beef)
1 egg
1 bunch chives
¼ teaspoon mild paprika
1 tablespoon tomato paste
150g (5oz) sour cream
salt and pepper
1 tablespoon oil
250ml (8fl oz) stock
1 teaspoon cornflour (cornstarch)
freshly ground pepper

Vegetables

A beautiful and tasty dish. These vegetables make a great accompaniment to many German dishes.

SERVES 6 – 8

KAROTTE, PASTINAK UND KOHL MIT SENFKÖRNERN

Carrot, Parsnip and Cabbage
with Mustard Seeds

Heat the oil in a frying pan and add the mustard seeds. They will start to pop instantly. Add the chilli and stir for approximately one minute.

Add the carrots, parsnips and cabbage. Toss over a medium heat for two to three minutes, then add parsley and mint and toss again.

Season with salt, freshly ground pepper and some sugar

Add lemon juice, then taste and correct seasoning. Serve immediately.

60ml (2fl oz) sunflower oil

1 tablespoon black mustard seeds

1 chilli, deseeded and chopped

225g (7½oz) carrots, coarsely grated

225g (7½oz) parsnips, grated

225g (7½oz) cabbage, finely shredded against grain

2 tablespoons parsley, chopped

2 tablespoons mint, freshly chopped

salt and freshly ground pepper

1 teaspoon sugar

2 tablespoons freshly-squeezed lemon juice, to taste

Slow cooked and rich in vibrant colour, this beautiful dish is sure to please! It makes an excellent accompaniment to roast pork or game. Vary the dish by using pears or a mix of apples and pears.

RINDFLEISCH ROULADEN

Braised Apple Red Cabbage

Pre-heat oven to a warm 160°C (325°F/ Gas Mark 3).

Cut the cabbage into quarters and cut out and discard the stalk. Finely shred the cabbage and place in a large saucepan of boiling water, ensuring there is enough water to cover the cabbage. Bring the water back to the boil and drain the cabbage. The cabbage will now appear an 'inky blue colour.' Don't be concerned, it will regain its colour at a later time when vinegar is added.

In a frying pan, sauté the onion in butter. Cook gently until transparent, then add the apple. Cook gently, stirring, for a further two to three minutes then remove from the pan and set aside.

Add the red cabbage and apple and onion mixture to an ovenproof casserole dish. Gently mix and layer together.

1 red cabbage

1 onion

butter

2 cooking apples, peeled, sliced and diced

2 teaspoons white or red wine vinegar

2 tablespoons water

1 tablespoon sugar

salt and pepper

Mix together the vinegar, water and sugar together and sprinkle over the dish. Note the red colour returning to cabbage as the vinegar is added. Season with salt and pepper.

Cover the cabbage with buttered, greaseproof paper and a lid and bake for one and a half hours or until tender. Ensure that the cabbage is stirred occasionally and moistened with a little extra water if necessary.

The cabbage should be both lightly sweet and sour. It may be necessary to add more sugar or vinegar to suit your taste and to achieve a wonderful result.

Refreshing and light. It's a great accompaniment to almost any German meal. A very popular dish of the 'homeland'.

GURKENSALAT

Cucumber Salad

2 medium cucumbers
1 ¼ cup red onion
1 tablespoon herbs, freshly chopped

DRESSING
125ml (4fl oz/ ½ cup) apple cider
    vinegar, wine vinegar
2 tablespoons oil
2–3 tablespoons sugar
salt and pepper, to taste

Peel and slice the cucumber to ¼cm (¹/₈in) thick and place on paper towel for 20 minutes to allow the water to wick out of the cucumber then place in bowl.

To make the dressing, simmer the vinegar in a saucepan. Stir in the oil and sugar and season. Allow to cool.

Add red onion to cucumber, then mix in the dressing and garnish with fresh herbs to serve.

Speck-Kartoffel Auflauf

Bacon and Potato Gratin

1 teaspoon sunflower oil

300g (10oz) bacon, diced

2 onions, diced

2 cloves garlic

2 tablespoons chopped flat-leaf
   parsley

1½ kg (3lb) potatoes

butter

2 teaspoons wholegrain mustard

250ml (8fl oz) pouring cream

salt and pepper

1 cup shredded tasty cheese

parsley

Pre-heat oven to 200°C (400°F/Gas Mark 5).

Heat the oil in a frying pan over medium heat and add the bacon to the pan and sauté until golden, about five minutes. Remove the bacon from the pan and set aside

Add the onion and garlic to pan and sauté until browned, about ten minutes. Set aside with the bacon and stir in the parsley.

Cut the potatoes in to ½cm (¼in) slices and layer in an ovenproof dish that has been greased with butter. Whilst layering the potatoes add the bacon, onion and parsley mixture.

Stir the wholegrain mustard into the cream and pour over the potatoes. Season with sea salt and grounded pepper.

Sprinkle the cheese over the top and cover with foil. Bake in the oven until cooked with the cheese is a golden colour. Garnish with more parsley and serve immediately.

Just delicious. A rustic salad, wholesome dish for summer.

Bohnen-Speck-Walnuß Salat

Green Bean, Bacon and Walnut Salad

750g (1½lb) green beans, trimmed
80g (3oz) walnuts
100g (3½oz) bacon, diced
3 cloves garlic, chopped
30g (1oz) sesame seeds
¾ cup flat-leaf parsley
2 teaspoons olive oil
40ml (1½fl oz) apple cider vinegar
salt and pepper

Bring a large pot of salted water to boil, add the beans and reduce the heat to medium and simmer until just tender, about 3 to 4 minutes. Drain and refresh under cold water and set aside.

Pre-heat the oven to 180°C (350°F/Gas Mark 4).

Place the walnuts on a small baking tray and roast until golden brown, approximately seven minutes, then allow to cool.

Sauté bacon and garlic over medium heat until cooked.

Place the walnuts, bacon, garlic, sesame seeds, olive oil and vinegar in a small mixing bowl.

Arrange the green beans onto a serving dish and gently spoon the mixture over the beans. Add the parsley. Season to taste and serve immediately.

Bacon or onion may be diced and added to this dish for an extra kick.

KRAÜTER KARTOFFELN

Mixed Herb Potatoes

Boil the potatoes in their jackets then allow to cool. Once cool dice into equal quarters.

In a frying pan heat the olive oil and add the potatoes, add a pinch of salt to taste and sprinkle over the mixed herbs. Cook until golden brown, turning the potatoes regularly to ensure all sides are browned.

Serve garnished with fresh herbs.

1½ kg (3lb) potatoes
125ml (4fl oz) olive oil
sea salt and pepper
1 teaspoon mixed dried herbs
fresh parsley or rosemary

This goes well with mashed or boiled potatoes and cooked greens on the side. Please note: You need to begin this recipe a day ahead.

BRAUNE BOHNEN MIT KNUSPRIGEN SCHINKEN

SERVES 4

Slow-baked Brown Beans with Roasted Bacon

2½ cups brown beans

1.25 kg (2lb 8oz) piece bacon

1 large brown onion, finely chopped

2 apples, peeled, cored and finely diced

100ml (3fl oz) balsamic vinegar

1/3 cup soft brown sugar

1 cinnamon stick, broken in half

2 garlic cloves, finely chopped

1½ teaspoons Hungarian sweet paprika

1 teaspoon dried marjoram

1½ teaspoons caraway seeds, lightly crushed

Soak the beans in a generous amount of water overnight.

Bring a large saucepan of water to the boil and add the piece of bacon. Bring back to the boil and cook steadily for one hour, then remove the bacon to a plate and reserve the liquid.

Pre-heat the oven to 170°C (350°F/Gas Mark 4). Drain the beans, then spread them in a large roasting tin with the onion. Pour in enough of the reserved cooking liquid to cover the beans, approximately three cups. Cover tightly with foil and cook in the oven for two and a half hours. Remove from the oven.

Stir in the apple, vinegar, sugar, cinnamon stick and garlic. Place a roasting rack over the top, making sure the rack does not touch the beans.

Remove the rind from the bacon so that the fat layer is exposed. Combine the paprika, marjoram and caraway and sprinkle over the top. Place bacon on the rack with the fat side facing up, and return to the oven.

Cook for 45 minutes, or until the bacon is very tender. If the beans are not saucy and thick by this stage, remove the bacon and keep warm.

Increase oven temperature to 200°C (400°F/ Gas Mark 5), and continue cooking for five to 10 minutes. Thickly slice the bacon and serve over the beans.

Photo on following page.

GEWÜRZTER JOGHURT-SOßE

Spiced Yoghurt Relish

1 red onion, thinly sliced
½ cucumber, deseeded and thinly sliced
1 tablespoon cumin seeds, toasted
1 bunch coriander (cilantro), roughly chopped (including stems)
2 tomatoes, quartered, deseeded and thinly sliced
400ml (13fl oz) plain full-fat yoghurt
salt and freshly ground black pepper

Combine onion and cucumber in a sieve, sprinkle generously with salt and set in bowl for ten minutes. Rinse thoroughly and pat dry.

Combine the cucumber and onion with the cumin seeds, coriander, tomatoes and yoghurt. Stir well and adjust the seasoning (usually there is enough salt from the cucumber and onion).

Cabbage has been known as poor man's fare, but it is such a glorious vegetable. It's low in cholestrol and rich in minerals, especially iron. This salad can be consumed hot or cold.

WEISSKOHL UND SPECK SALAT

White Cabbage and Bacon Salad

1 white cabbage
100ml (3fl oz) olive oil
125ml (4fl oz/ ½ cup) white wine vinegar
375ml (12fl oz/ 1½ cups) warm water
1 teaspoon caraway seeds
50ml (1½fl oz) white wine
3 rashes bacon or speck, diced
salt and pepper

Quarter the cabbage and remove the stalk, then wash thoroughly in salted water and drain well.

Cut the cabbage into fine strips and place in a large bowl. Add the olive oil and mix throughout cabbage and let stand for one hour.

Mix the vinegar, warm water, caraway seeds and wine together well and pour this over the cabbage. Cover for one to two hours.

Sauté the bacon in a pan until golden and add this to the cabbage salad, mix thoroughly and season to taste.

This would go well with almost any dish. Vary the vegetables used and add fresh garden herbs to garnish and create that rustic, home-cooked fare that will tempt and delight the eye.

SERVES 4

WINTERLICHES GEMÜSE IN WEIßWEINSOßE

Winter Vegetable *in (German Riesling) White Wine*

Heat the oil in a large frying pan over medium heat, add bacon and cook until golden brown. Lower the heat and add the spring onions and a pinch of salt. Cook for a further two minutes.

Add the carrots, celery and zucchini then pour wine and chicken stock over the vegetables. Cook and reduce over medium heat. Add tomato and cook for a further 5 to 10 minutes.

In two separate saucepans gently boil green beans and peas until semi-cooked. Drain and refresh in iced water

Add green beans and peas to the other vegetables and simmer for a further three to five minutes.

Garnish with fresh garden herbs and serve with potato mash or gratin and your favourite meat.

2 tablespoons olive oil

100g (3½oz) bacon hock or smoked leg ham

3 spring onions (scallions), sliced into batons

salt

1 large carrot, peeled and sliced into batons

1 celery

1 zucchini (courgette)

1 cup fresh peas

250g (8oz) fresh green beans

2 fresh diced tomatoes

100ml (3fl oz) Riesling or white wine

100ml (3fl oz) homemade chicken stock

fresh herbs

Rösti can be served with smoked salmon and dill and caper dressing or with fresh apple sauce as a sweet treat.

MAKES 12 RÖSTI

KARTOFFEPUFFER

Potato Rösti

Peel and finely grate the potatoes. Place them into a fresh clean tea towel and squeeze out any moisture.

Combine the cream, egg yolk and grated potato in a bowl, then season with salt and pepper and nutmeg. Form 12 potato cakes.

Heat the oil over medium heat in a shallow pan and fry the cakes, flattening each cake with a spatula and cooking both sides until they are golden.

800g (1¾lbs) potatoes
100g (3½oz) fresh cream
1 egg yolk
salt and freshly ground pepper
nutmeg
4 tablespoons oil

Dressings & Sauces

Great with fish and prawn dishes accompanied by fresh garden salads.

SCHNITTLAUCH-ZITRONEN SENFDRESSING

MAKES 150ML/4 1/2FL OZ

Fresh Chive, Lemon and *Dijon Mustard Dressing*

80ml (2½fl oz) lemon juice
150ml (5fl oz) extra virgin olive oil
1½ tablespoons Dijon mustard
2 tablespoons fresh chives, chopped
1 garlic clove, finely chopped
salt and pepper, to taste

Blend all the ingredients in a blender until combined.

Great with goats' cheese salad and beans and baked beetroot.

KAPERNSOSSE

MAKES 150ML/41/2FL OZ

Caper Dressing

1½ tablespoons red wine vinegar
200ml (7fl oz) olive oil
3 garlic cloves, crushed
1½ tablespoons capers
sea salt and pepper

Whisk all ingredients in a small bowl until blended. Use immediately.

This dressing is delicious poured over hot and cold vegetables and salad. It is particularly yummy as a warm potato dressing.

MAKES APPROX. 400ML/13FL OZ

Catherine's Speziell Salatsoße

Catherine's Special Salad Dressing

Whisk all ingredients in a small bowl until blended. Use immediately.

2 free-range eggs
3 tablespoons wholegrain mustard
125ml (4fl oz/ ½ cup) red wine
  vinegar
¼ teaspoon paprika
1 teaspoon white sugar
250ml (8fl oz/ 1 cup) grapeseed oil
sea salt, to taste
1 teaspoon mayonnaise

MEERRETTISCH SOßE

Horseradish Dressing

Whisk all ingredients in a small bowl until blended.
Use immediately.

¾ cup horseradish

3 teaspoons Dijon mustard

3 teaspoons chopped horseradish

1 tablespoon lemon juice

2 tablespoons water

AIOLI

Aioli

1 egg yolk
1 clove garlic, crushed
1 teaspoon Dijon mustard
1 teaspoon white wine vinegar
250ml (8fl oz/ 1 cup) olive oil
1 teaspoon lemon juice

Combine egg yolk, garlic, mustard and white wine vinegar in a blender.

Gradually add the olive oil in a thin steady stream. Blend until the aioli thickens then add the lemon juice.

Desserts

A beautiful dessert on a hot day. This is a particularly popular dessert in Germany. Everyone just loves it—children especially.

FRUCHTPUDDING

Fruit Pudding

SERVES 6

250g (8oz) red currants
125g (4oz) strawberries
125g (4oz) red cherries
1 tablespoon sugar
2 tablespoons cornflour (cornstarch)

Wash the fruit and remove stems. Add fruits to a saucepan, along with a little bit of water and the sugar. Cook gently for ten minutes.

Mix the cornflour with a little bit of cold water then add in to the fruit mixture. Allow it to cook for two minutes more to thicken.

Allow to cool slightly. Fill dessert dishes or glasses and place in the refrigerator to cool completely.

Serve with warm vanilla sauce or vanilla ice-cream.

Germany is a cake-loving country and this cake is vert popular around Christmas. This cake is perfect served with fresh coffe.

ROTWEINKUCHEN

Red Wine Cake

4 eggs
250g (8oz) flour
2 level teaspoons vanilla sugar
2½ level teaspoons baking powder
200g (7oz) sugar
250g (8oz) butter
¹/3 cup cinnamon
1–2 tablespoons cocoa
125ml (4fl oz) red wine
100g (3½oz) grated chocolate

Pre-heat the oven to 180°C (350°F/Gas Mark 4). Mix together all ingredients except the eggs and chocolate.

Separate the eggs, add the yolks into the mixture and then beat the egg whites until stiff. Fold in the grated chocolate and then mix gently in to the mixture.

Place in a greased cake pan and bake for 50 to 60 minutes.

My mother used to bake this for afternoon tea, to share with her neighbours when they met for coffee on a Sunday.

SERVES 8-10

MUTTI'S KAFFEEKUCHEN

Mother's Coffee Cake

Pre-heat the oven to 180°C (350°F/Gas Mark 4). Mix the filling ingredients together and set aside.

To make the cake, beat the butter until fluffy, gradually add the sugar and vanilla sugar then add one egg at a time. Mix in the flour and baking powder then add the cream.

Put a third of the dough in an oiled and flour-dusted cake tray. Spread half of the filling over it. Take another third of the cake mixture and place on top of the filling then layer on the last of the filling and then the last of the cake mix on top.

Use a fork to fold the mixture in one twist to form a slight pattern then bake for 60 minutes

After it has cooked, leave it to cool for 10 minutes before you take it out of the tin.

If you like, decorate with chocolate icing or dust the top with icing sugar.

250g (8oz) butter or margarine
300g (10oz) sugar
2 teaspoons vanilla sugar
2 eggs
350g (11oz) plain (all-purpose) flour
2 teaspoons baking powder
200g (7oz) cream

FILLING
150g (5oz) brown sugar
125g (4oz) walnut meal
1 teaspoon cinnamon

My mother would make this for me as a child. It is an afternoon treat for the whole family to enjoy.

KALTER HUND

Cold Dog

Chop the dark chocolate into small pieces and heat it up in a saucepan over low heat with the coconut oil, stirring constantly until melted. Add the icing sugar, almonds and milk chocolate and mix in.

Line a rectangular cake tin (20cm/8in) long) with aluminium foil. Lay enough of the scotch fingers in to cover the bottom, then pour over a layer of the chocolate mixture approximately 2cm (3/4in) deep. Repeat the layers until all the mixture is used.

Leave it in the refrigerator for about three hours. Remove from the tin and slice to serve. Cut gently to ensure the biscuits do not crumble.

100g (3½oz) dark chocolate
125g (4oz) coconut oil
75g (3oz) icing sugar
40g (1½oz) almonds, chopped
2 tablespoons milk chocolate, chopped
15 scotch finger biscuits

Just delicious served with custard. Lovely to bake for an afternoon break with family and good friends.

SERVES 8—10

Chocolate and Cinnamon Cherry Cake

Pre-heat oven to 180°C (350°F) Gas Mark 4.

Beat the eggs, vanilla sugar and half of the caster sugar together in a mixing bowl until frothy.

Add the other half of the sugar, the sunflower oil, cocoa powder and flour. Mix in the baking powder and chocolate until well blended then add the sour cherries and cinnamon.

Use butter and extra flour in a round cake tin and pour in the cake mixture.

Bake for around 60 minutes or until cooked.

4 free-range eggs

15g (¹/₂oz) vanilla sugar

150g (5 oz) caster (superfine) sugar

150ml (4¹/₂fl oz) sunflower oil

4 tablespoons cocoa powder

300g (10oz) flour, plus
* 2 tablespoons extra*

15g (¹/₂oz) baking pocwder

100g (3¹/₂oz) chocolate chip bits

500g (1lb) sour cherries, drained

1 teaspoon cinnamon

1 tablespoon butter

A great combination of ingredients and very simple to make—very decadent.

Pochierten Feigen in Dunkel Schokoladensoße

Dark Chocolate *with* Port Wine Poached Figs

200g (7oz) dark chocolate
425ml (15fl oz) custard
6–8 fresh figs
200ml (7fl oz) port wine
100g (3¹/₂oz) caster (superfine)
  sugar
white chocolate, to serve

Place serving glasses or ramekins in the freezer to chill.

Melt the chocolate by placing in a heat-proof bowl set over a saucepan of gently simmering water. Stir gently until the chocolate has melted, this will take about three or so minutes. Remove from the heat.

Pour a third of the custard into the melted chocolate and mix gently until the chocolate mixture thickens, be careful not to over mix. Pour in the remaining custard and stir, the mixture will thicken as it cools.

Spoon the mixture into the chilled serving ramekins or glasses and put them back into the freezer to further chill until set, usually 20 to 30 minutes or so.

To prepare the poached figs, wash and quarter the figs and put them in a saucepan with the port wine and sugar. Gently bring to a simmer over a low heat until thickened.

Cool then divide among the chilled glasses and grate white chocolate over the top. Serve chilled.

This cake is well known in East Germany and can only be bought in Freiberg and surrounds. The legend goes it was originally a cheesecake, but there was no more curd left in the area, as the townspeople had used it to build the city wall. So they baked it without, creating the Freiberger Eierschecke.

FREIBERGER EIERSCHECKE

SERVES 4

Freiberger Cheesecake

For the dough:
500g (1lb) flour
150g (5oz) sugar
80g (3oz) margarine
1 pinch salt
250ml (9oz) milk, lukewarm
30g (1oz) yeast
some vanilla sugar
some lemon zest

For the filling:
150g (5oz) egg yolk (about six eggs)
150g (5oz) caster (superfine) sugar
150g (5oz) softened butter
handful of raisins, for sprinkling
flaked almonds for sprinkling

Firstly, prepare the yeast dough. Place the flour in a bowl. Spread the edge of the bowl with sugar, margarine and salt and zest.

Whisk the crumbled yeast, 1 teaspoon of sugar and half of the lukewarm milk then pour into a well in the centre of the bowl. Stir in enough flour to make a small, firm dough. Dust dough with flour, then cover and put in a warm place for about 20 minutes. Knead all ingredients together and put it back to the warm place. After about 45 minutes knead again and roll out onto a greased baking sheet and prick several times with a fork. Cover and allow to rise for 15 minutes.

For the filling, beat the egg yolk and sugar until creamy. Add butter, bit by bit, and mix all together to make a creamy mixture. Spread onto the yeast dough. Sprinkle with raisins and flaked almonds.

Bake at 160°C (325°F/Gas Mark 3) for about 15–20 minutes.

These are very typical German Christmas Cookies. They are also very popular to eat the whole year round.

KOKOSMAKRONEN

Christmas Cookies

4 egg whites

250g (8oz) sugar

120g (4oz) coconut flakes

baking or edible wafers (4cm/ ½in)
in diameter)

2 teaspoons lemon zest, grated

250g (8oz) chocolate, melted, for
decoration (optional)

Prepare a water bath, by heating water in a tray. In a bowl, mix egg whites and sugar. Place the bowl in the hot water bath and beat the eggs and sugar until the sugar dissolves.

Mix in the coconut flakes. Heat the coconut mixture to a temperature of 70°C (158°F), stirring frequently.

Remove from the water bath, add flour and mix again. If you like you can add the grated lemon zest to this mixture. Let cool to room temperature again. Pre-heat oven to 160°C (325°F). Place baking wafers on baking tray.

Use an icing bag with large opening to place little dough dollops on the wafers. Leave a little rim, because while baking the cookies will flatten slightly. Bake for 10 minutes. Then open the oven a little bit and bake for another 5 minutes. The cookies should remain light in colour and just slightly browned.

If you would like, you can decorate the cookies with melted chocolate. Break the chocolate up into small pieces and place in a bowl over the water bath. Stir until it has just melted. Take the bowl out of water bath. Dip the cookies into the chocolate to coat the top.

Note: These cookies are baked on thin, edible baking wafers, known as oblaten. Baking wafers are a crisp, white wheat wafer, similar to communion wafers. Check your local specialty store. You could also try edible rice wafers instead (available from cake decorating stores) or just grease your baking tray before placing the cookie mixture on to the tray.

Acknowledgements

The recipes collected in this book are our family favourites. To me, German food means homestyle cooking, food cooked with love.

It is with love and heartfelt gratitude that I acknowledge my wife—contributor and supporter—in this book's creation. The love and encouragement from my three daughters is also much appreciated. A special thanks to Bella for all her hard work with typing the manuscript.

To my mother, who taught me to cook with heart, and develop a passion for food. To Hans—you were an inspiration who led me to follow in your footsteps. Special mention and thanks to my father, whose appreciation of food is second to none. To Katya, our restaurant manager—thank you for your beautiful dessert recipes. Finally to all at New Holland. Sincere thanks to you for giving me the opportunity to share 'my German kitchen' with others.

Index of Recipes

a note on measurements
1 tablespoon equals 20ml (or 4 teaspoons)
1 teaspoon equals 5ml
1 cup equals 250ml

First published 2012 by
New Holland Publishers Pty Ltd
London • Sydney • Cape Town • Auckland

Garfield House 86–88 Edgware Road London W2 2EA United Kingdom
1/66 Gibbes Street Chatswood NSW 2067 Australia
218 Lake Road Northcote Auckland New Zealand
Wembley Square First Floor Solan Road Gardens Cape Town 8001 South Africa

www.newhollandpublishers.com
www.newholland.com.au

A record of this book is held at the National Library of Australia and the British Library.

ISBN 9781742572536

Publisher: Fiona Schultz
Publishing director: Lliane Clarke
Designer: Tracy Loughlin
Editor: Kay Proos
Proofreader: Catherine Etteridge
Project editor: Jodi De Vantier
Food Photography: Graeme Gillies
Food stylist: Bhavani Konings
Production director: Olga Dementiev
Printer: Toppan Leefung Printing Limited

10 9 8 7 6 5 4 3 2 1

Keep up with New Holland Publishers on Facebook and Twitter
www.facebook.com/NewHollandPublishers